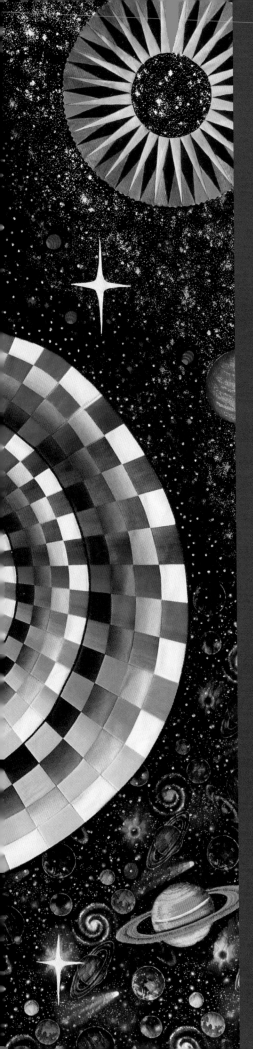

SECTION TWO
More Possibilities 39

Chapter 4   Semi-Circle Weaving (Banana Shaped) *Inspiration* . . 40

Chapter 5   Circle Curvy Weaving *Inspiration* 42

Chapter 6   Diagonal Weaving *Inspiration* 44

Chapter 7   Combination Weaving *Inspiration* 46

Chapter 8   Combination of Shredded Blocks and
             Circle Curvy Weaving *Inspiration* 50

Chapter 9   Partly Curvy Weaving *Inspiration* 52

Chapter 10   Circle and Spiral Weaving with Two
             Hand-Painted Fabrics *Inspiration* 54

Chapter 11   Fuzzy Weaving *Inspiration* 62

             Basic Instructions. 66
             About the Author. 70

Foreword

Anna Faustino showed her quilts at the meetings of two quilting guilds I belong to: Jersey City Quilters and Empire Quilters in New York City. She introduced herself and said she had painted prior to quilting. As she showed us her quilts, we were amazed and awed. Her work has an uncanny beauty. I knew then that she was a truly gifted quilt artist. Needless to say, people reacted to Anna's work with words like "stunning, truly original, dazzling, gorgeous, riotous color, a visual delight, eye candy, and exciting." People have a physical response to Anna's creations: they move you, lift your spirits, and make you soar.

After the meeting, I asked Anna about her plans and hopes for her magnificent work. She had a vision for her work, and she said she dreamed of writing a book. I told her that she could accomplish anything she put her mind to. Well, she ultimately got the opportunity to write the book she dreamed of.

Anna's art quilts are a result of hard work, commitment, passion, top-notch design, great color combinations, and beautiful planning. She is meticulous in her attention to detail and her technique. Anna has exhibited her quilts regionally, nationally, and internationally and has won numerous awards.

In this book, Anna gives complete instructions for three projects and guidance for over twenty of her quilts. Anna is a great teacher. Her students all rave about the experience of taking one of her classes. Don't be intimidated because weaving quilts is so different from anything you may have attempted before in quilting. The concept of weaving is easy, and the results will simply astonish you. So enjoy yourself and be prepared for an unexpected treat when you take a class with Anna Faustino through this wonderful book.

Your life as a quilter will never be the same. I promise.

Sandra Samaniego
Avid quilter and big fan

Your life as a quilter will never be the same.

SIMPLY STUNNING
Woven Quilts

Anna Faustino

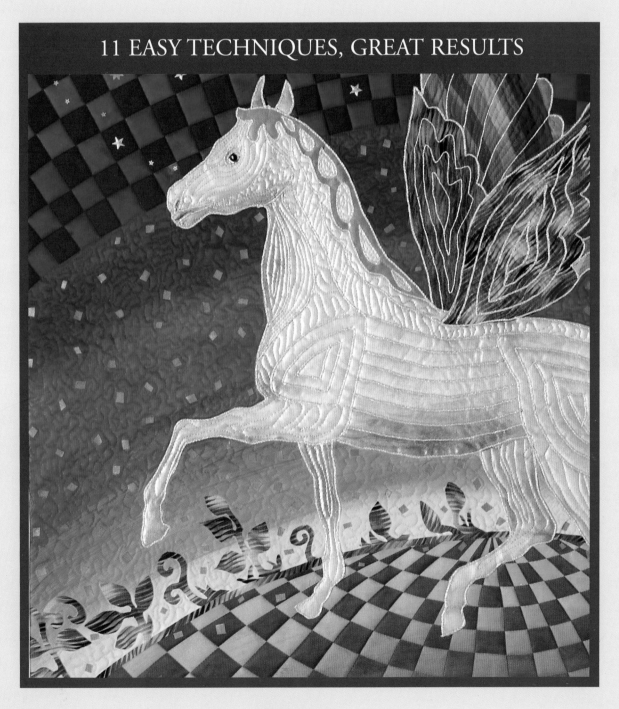

11 EASY TECHNIQUES, GREAT RESULTS

C&T PUBLISHING

Text copyright © 2008 by Anna Faustino

Artwork copyright © 2008 by C&T Publishing, Inc., and Anna Faustino

PUBLISHER: *Amy Marson*

EDITORIAL DIRECTOR: *Gailen Runge*

ACQUISITIONS EDITOR: *Jan Grigsby*

EDITOR: *Liz Aneloski*

TECHNICAL EDITORS: *Teresa Stroin and Jane Miller*

COPYEDITOR/PROOFREADER: *Wordfirm Inc.*

COVER DESIGNER: *Kristy K. Zacharias*

BOOK DESIGNER: *Rose Sheifer-Wright*

PRODUCTION COORDINATOR: *Matthew Allen*

ILLUSTRATOR: *Anna Faustino and Kirstie L. Pettersen*

PHOTOGRAPHY BY *Luke Mulks and Diane Pedersen* of C&T Publishing, unless otherwise noted

Published by C&T Publishing, Inc., P.O. Box 1456, Lafayette, CA 94549

Library of Congress Cataloging-in-Publication Data

Faustino, Anna

  Simply stunning woven quilts : 11 easy techniques, great results / Anna Faustino.

       p. cm.

  Includes index.

  ISBN 978-1-57120-452-3 (paper trade : alk. paper)

  1. Patchwork–Patterns. 2. Strip quilting–Patterns. 3. Hand weaving–Patterns. I. Title.

  TT835.F378 2008

  746.46'041–dc22

              2007028871

Printed in China

10 9 8 7 6 5 4 3 2 1

Dedication

This book is dedicated to my husband, Ismael Candido Pereira Faustino. He is not only my husband but my dearest, best friend and the greatest partner. Through happy times and hard times, he is always there for me with an open heart and a big warm hug. His understanding of my passion to make quilts is absolutely amazing. I thank him for his love, support, and encouragement and for being the most important, and certainly the best, part of my life.

Contents

Foreword. 6
Acknowledgments. 7
Introduction 9

SECTION ONE
Techniques and Projects
to Get You Started 11

Chapter 1   Simple Curvy Weaving 12
Project: *Spring Flowers*. 13
Inspiration. 19

Chapter 2   Woven Shredded Blocks 22
Project: *Apple Power* 23
Inspiration. 29

Chapter 3   Circle Weaving 32
Project: *Color Wheel* 33
Inspiration. 38

Acknowledgments

I'd like to express my thanks to the following individuals: First and foremost, to my husband, who believed in me and, with his words and actions, supported me every step of the way. He always told me that I could do it. I must thank him officially for allowing me to take over our living spaces with my fabrics, sewing machines, and hundreds of papers while working on this book—also for giving me his large shoulders to cry on.

To my son, Andrew, whose sense of humor made me laugh, even from far away. He is always full of ideas and ready to share them with everybody. I have learned from him how to think positively and be optimistic.

To the members of the Warwick Valley Quilting Guild, who gave me a standing ovation (for the first time, I must say), giving me a sense of pride and accomplishment, and a boost to go forward.

To the members of Empire Quilters, who, from the moment that I mentioned I was thinking about writing a book, never stopped telling me to go for it and made me feel proud of my quilts every time they saw them.

To my friend Sandra Samaniego, who told me I should write a book and gave me moral support and help when I needed it. Every time I spoke with her, I felt energized and recharged.

To Liz Aneloski, my developmental editor, who with a stroke of a pen can make everything sound so much better. I thank her for her understanding and for answering all my questions during the process.

To Jan Grigsby, who first called me to tell me that C&T Publishing had accepted my proposal and agreed to publish my book. The news made me so happy that I cried and thanked her a million times.

To all the C&T Publishing team, without whom this book would not have been possible.

To my workshop students, who gave me words of encouragement and always a feeling of accomplishment.

To Carol Taylor, who encouraged me to write the book by admiring my work and telling me to pursue my dreams.

To Caryl Bryer Fallert, for her beautiful fabrics, which I love. They make my quilting a joy, and they fit perfectly into my techniques, especially her Gradations collection for Benartex.

To Marie and Jose Loureiro, for their fabric support and all the time they spent looking at and discussing my artwork.

Anna

Introduction

Many people are interested in and involved with art and creativity. They want to learn professional teachers' and artists' secrets for making beautiful works of art. In reality, professionals succeed not because they have secrets (although they do discover tips and tricks) but because they are constantly experimenting, observing, and memorizing surrounding objects and nature, and studying the details and colors of the beauty of our world, and life.

The road to high artistry is a journey. Reaching your artistic goals takes experimentation and practice. If you have the interest and patience, you will have many happy hours and days in your life.

Art quilting allows us to express ourselves and gives us satisfaction through the use of designs, colors, fabrics, and threads. Don't be afraid to make experimental quilts—try different things, create new embellishments, use different materials, and combine techniques and materials in different ways. Learn from your mistakes and let your work evolve; every piece will be better than the previous.

> *Weaving is the art of forming a fabric by interlacing at right angles two or more sets of yarn or other materials....*
>
> *Weaving is one of the most ancient fundamental arts. In the tombs and ruins of Egypt and Peru, among cliff and lake dwellers' relics, and in the most ancient picture records, are found the tools, materials, and story of textile craftsmanship.*
>
> —*Illustrated Colombia Encyclopedia*

On a cold and rainy day seven or eight years ago, I was flipping channels on the television and became interested in the *Simply Quilts* program hosted by Alex Anderson. For several years, I collected a stash of fabrics and recorded hundreds of hours of the program. In 2004, I started to make quilts from book patterns like New York Beauty, and I learned techniques like stitch and flip, and colorwash bargello. Quiltmaking was fun, and I was hooked. I subscribed to Fons and Porter's magazine *Love of Quilting*, where I learned about and entered a Log Cabin contest. The thought of this competition kept me sleepless for a week. After I read the entry rules, I began thinking of options and variations to make a unique quilt. Inspiration gave me colorful images. As I looked at my sketches, I realized that I could develop a new technique by combining traditional Log Cabin blocks with weaving. The project instructions beginning on page 23 will walk you through the process.

TECHNIQUES AND PROJECTS TO GET YOU STARTED

CHAPTER 1

SIMPLE CURVY WEAVING

The *Spring Flowers* project will show you how to use the simple curvy weaving technique to create the background for a quilt; there are no seams, blocks, or patches. The quilt is made from two pieces of fabric cut into curvy strips and then woven together. Appliqué and embellishments can be added on top.

Try this technique for yourself. The following project will walk you through the process step-by-step. Make the quilt as it is presented or change the colors, details, and textures to add your own personality and character.

SPRING FLOWERS

SPRING FLOWERS

Finished quilt size: 19½" × 19½"

I created this small quilt project to help you understand the concept of weaving. I chose colorful fabrics with gradated colors that complement one another.

Fabric samples

MATERIALS

Fabric amounts are based on 40" fabric width. Prewash all fabrics before use.

- Pink-purple (A): ¾ yard
- Yellow-green (B): ¾ yard
- Orange: approximately 6" × 10" for basket
- Light, medium, and dark green scraps: at least 3" × 3" for each leaf
- Tulle: ¾ yard*
- Backing: ¾ yard
- Cotton batting: 24" × 24"
- Binding: ⅓ yard
- Transparent thread
- Various thread colors for appliqué and quilting
- Paper-backed fusible adhesive (I use 17"-wide HeatnBond Lite by Therm O Web): 2 yards
- 90 small silk flowers (OR enough flowered fabric to cut out flowers to cover the space, as shown in the appliqué placement diagram on page 17)
- Marking pencils for dark and light fabrics (erasable or water-soluble)
- Permanent fabric markers: brown, red, orange
- Beads
- Masking tape

*Optional depending on raw edge finishing technique (Step 18, Page 16)

CUTTING

Pink-purple fabric (A): Cut a square 20½" × 20½".

Yellow-green fabric (B): Cut a square 20½" × 20½".

WOVEN BACKGROUND

1. Cut pieces of fusible adhesive large enough to completely cover fabrics A and B. Following the manufacturer's instructions, fuse the adhesive to the wrong sides of the fabrics.

2. Remove the paper backing from both pieces. (You may want to save it to use as a pressing sheet for another project.)

3. Place the pre-fused fabric A right side up on a cutting mat. With a water-soluble or erasable marking pencil, draw vertical and horizontal center lines. Then draw a vertical line ¾" to the right of the center line and another vertical line ¾" to the left of the center line. Draw 5 more vertical lines 1½" apart on each side of the center line.

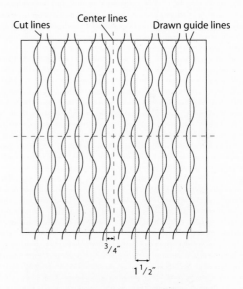

Cut lines   Center lines   Drawn guide lines

¾"

1½"

Mark center and vertical lines on fabric.
Don't draw the curvy lines; cut them.

4. Place the pre-fused fabric B right side up on the cutting mat and draw vertical and horizontal center lines. Draw horizontal lines 1½" apart, placing the first 2 lines ¾" away from the center line, as you did in Step 3 for the vertical lines.

Note

Don't draw the curvy lines shown in the photo and illustration; these are guide lines to help you see how to cut the curvy strips.

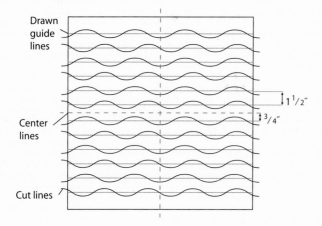

Drawn guide lines

Center lines

Cut lines

1½"

¾"

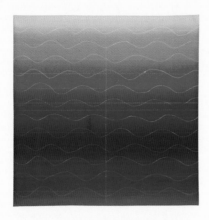

Mark center and horizontal lines on fabric.
Don't draw the curvy lines; cut them.

5. Place masking tape ½" from the top edge of fabric A (to prevent cutting through this section).

6. Starting with the vertical center strip on fabric A, freehand cut curvy strips with a rotary cutter. Cross the drawn straight lines with gentle curves, approximately ½" to the left and right of the lines. Cut from the bottom edge of the fabric toward the masking tape and stop at the tape. (Do not cut through the tape.) Make one cut on the right of center, then one on the left, then one on the right, and so on until all the strips are cut.

Note

When using a rotary cutter, always cut away from your body. If you're not confident of your skill, practice on scrap fabric first.

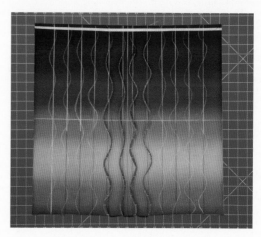

Cut fabric A into vertical curvy strips.

Note

If you cut through the masking tape by mistake, don't worry. We snip these ends apart later anyway. Just pin them tightly next to each other as if they had never been cut.

7. There are 2 options for cutting the fabric B strips.

Option 1

Cut fabric B into curvy strips crossing the horizontal lines, starting from the center strip as you did for fabric A. Number each strip so you can keep them in the proper order. (Start with the center strip and number strips 1–6 below it going down. Number strips 7–12 above the center strip going up.)

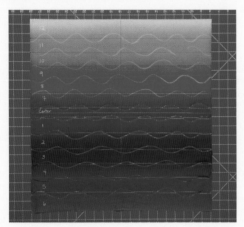

Number the fabric B strips before cutting horizontal curvy strips.

Option 2

Cut 1 strip of fabric B, starting from the center strip as you did for fabric A. Weave it into fabric A (Step 9). Cut the next strip of fabric B, weave it into fabric A, and so on.

8. Place the 24″ × 24″ cotton batting on a weaving pad (page 66). Pin fabric A (above the masking tape) to the weaving pad, centering the fabric on top of the batting.

9. Weave the center strip of fabric B into the horizontal center of fabric A—over, under, over, under and so on—and pin the fabric B strip on the sides. As you weave, make sure to align the center line drawn on the fabric B strip with the horizontal center line drawn across the vertical strips of fabric A.

Each fabric B strip starts either over or under the outer fabric A strip. Alternate "over" rows with "under" rows.

10. Weave the next strip of fabric B into fabric A below the first fabric B strip: under, over, under, over, and so on, and pin it on the sides. Keep the woven strips close to each other. Repeat with the third strip.

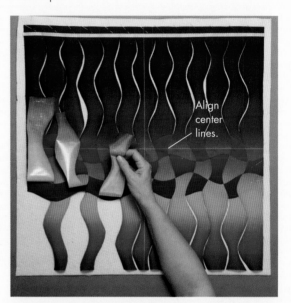
Align center lines.

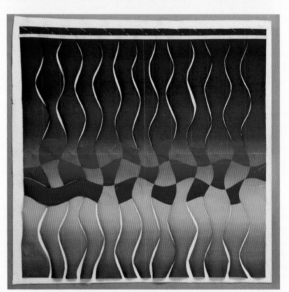

Weave fabric B strips into fabric A and pin.

11. Continue weaving and pinning strips. Pin the last horizontal strip on the bottom to the very end of each vertical strip.

Use all-metal pins. This allows you to iron over the pins after the weaving is finished to fuse it sufficiently so it won't come apart when the pins are removed. Take the pins out and press again.

Continue weaving strips and pinning.

12. Rotate the weaving pad 180°. Remove the masking tape and unpin the uncut section of fabric A at the unwoven end of the vertical strips. Finish cutting the vertical curvy strips by snipping the ends to separate the strips from one another.

Rotate 180°, remove tape, unpin, and snip
strip ends in uncut section.

13. Rotate the remaining fabric B strips 180° and weave them into fabric A, pinning on the sides, as you did for the first half of the fabric B strips. Pin the last strip to every vertical strip.

Rotate fabric B strips, weave them into fabric A, and pin.

14. The woven piece should be square. Adjust the strips gently toward the center—make them fit tightly at the intersections.

15. Following the fusible adhesive manufacturer's instructions, fuse the woven piece to the batting. Start from the center and press (lift up and down)—do not slide the iron.

Fuse to batting.

16. Remove the pins. Iron again to ensure that the weaving is completely fused.

17. Place the quilt top on the cutting mat and trim it to 20″ × 20″ square.

18. Choose Option 1, 2, or 3 (page 67) to finish the raw edges of the woven strips.

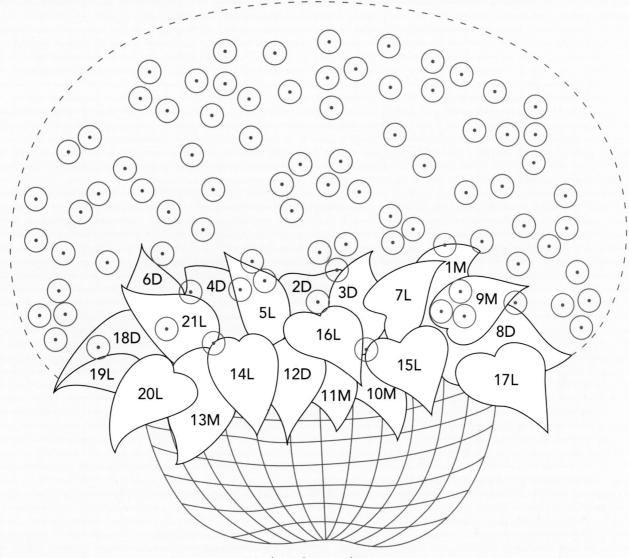

Appliqué placement diagram

APPLIQUÉ

1. Place paper-backed fusible adhesive on top of the appliqué patterns on the pullout page (paper side up, adhesive side down), and attach it with masking tape. Trace the basket and all the leaves onto the paper side of the fusible adhesive. The patterns are reversed and ready to trace. Label the leaves with their corresponding number and letter labels. If a leaf has 2 labels, trace it twice—once for each label.

2. Cut out the shapes approximately ¼" outside the drawn lines.

3. Fuse the traced leaves to the wrong side of the green fabrics, referring to the L (light green), M (medium green), and D (dark green) labels. Fuse the traced basket to the wrong side of the orange fabric.

4. Cut out the appliqué pieces on the drawn lines.

5. Referring to the appliqué placement diagram, position all the appliqué pieces (the basket first, then the leaves in numerical order) on the quilt top. Remove the paper backing as you place each piece. When you are happy with your composition, follow the fusible adhesive manufacturer's instructions to fuse the composition to the quilt. Make sure the iron is not too hot.

6. Randomly place the silk flowers in the area inside the dashed line shown on the appliqué placement diagram.

7. If the flowers are from a craft shop or scrapbooking store, they may already have adhesive on the back. If they don't have adhesive or if you are using flowers cut from fabric, put paper-backed fusible adhesive on them first; then cut and fuse them to the quilt.

8. Draw the texture lines in the basket using permanent fabric markers.

9. If you are covering your quilt with tulle, do so now (page 67).

10. Use a zigzag stitch with transparent thread to couch embroidery floss onto the basket (page 67). Satin stitch with matching thread around the leaves and any large fabric flowers you may have added.

QUILTING AND FINISHING

1. Layer, baste, and quilt. Quilt in-the-ditch along the weaving lines of the background and around the appliqué using transparent thread. Use variegated thread to quilt short lines from the centers of the flowers for stems and use green thread for the vein lines in the leaves.

2. After quilting, hand embellish the small flowers with beads. If you used larger fabric flowers, embellish as desired.

3. Refer to pages 68–69 for binding instructions.

These flowers were cut from print fabric to use for appliqué.

Inspiration

The discovery of Tutankhamen's tomb opened a new chapter in the art and history of the world. Now we can actually see Tutankhamen's golden mask and appreciate the beauty of preserved youth. Egyptian art always inspires me.

The first quilt I made with a woven background was *Golden Treasure*. I chose two quilt-size pieces of fabrics in colors of the desert and sand for the background. I cut both fabrics in curvy strips and wove them together using the simple curvy weaving technique beginning on page 12.

The woven background in this quilt complements the appliqué, showing added depth, movement, and interest and awakening the imagination. I used many gold fabrics, in different textures, and gold yarns. I wanted to show the pharaoh's eyes bringing a message from the past.

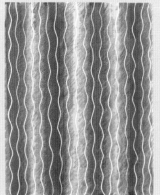
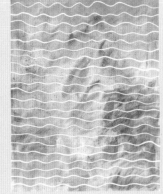

Fabrics cut into curvy strips

GOLDEN TREASURE, 42½" × 43"

STAYING ALIVE, 37 ½" × 24 ½"

I made *Staying Alive* to raise awareness about the fight against the poisoning of the earth and its waters with mercury. Fish can fight against the current but not against an ingestion of mercury.

I made this quilt from sateen fabric that was hand dyed, hand painted, and hand stamped. The background is woven from two quilt-size pieces of the sateen fabric: one with the lengthwise grain running in the vertical direction and the other with the lengthwise grain running in the horizontal direction. I cut both pieces in curvy strips and wove the strips together using the simple curvy weaving technique beginning on page 12. The shiny fabric created a beautiful water-effect, and you can see a color play when you change the angle from which you look at the quilt. The fish are fused, machine appliquéd, and embellished with couching.

Fabrics cut into curvy strips

THREE GRACES, 29" × 47"

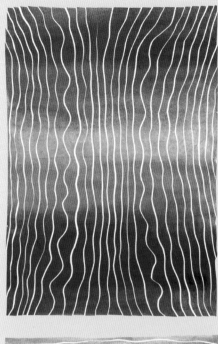

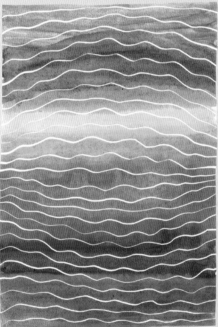

Fabrics cut into curvy strips

Using the simple curvy weaving technique beginning on page 12, I created a woven background for the cheery appliquéd sunflowers in *Three Graces*. I pieced together 2 panels of variegated fabrics, then wove them together. Even though I used only three fabrics for the background, there appear to be many more, owing to the variety of colors in the variegated fabrics. You can see different areas of sky and ground. Creating this quilt was an interesting experience. I enjoy interpreting beautiful things in the world. When you design your quilts, be sure to add personality and character, color, details, and texture.

CHAPTER 2

WOVEN SHREDDED BLOCKS

The woven shredded blocks technique was the beginning for this entire book. I discovered that I could combine traditional Log Cabin construction with weaving. The result of this experiment surprised me so much that I started to manipulate different weaving techniques with other basic blocks. You can use the shredded blocks technique with most pieced blocks. *Apple Power* will walk you through the process step-by-step.

APPLE POWER

APPLE POWER

Finished quilt size: 21" × 21"

For this project, you will create two identical 22" × 22" Log Cabin blocks in two color palettes, cut them into strips, and weave them together. The process is a little challenging—it's like cutting blocks apart and putting them back together as a puzzle. Some accuracy is required, but I know you can do it.

MATERIALS

Fabric amounts are based on 40" fabric width.

Prewash all fabrics before use.

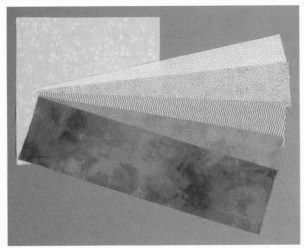

6 fabrics for Log Cabin block A

6 fabrics for Log Cabin block B

- 6 yellow to orange fabrics for block A
  (*fabrics are listed from lightest to darkest*):
  Fabric 1A: 6½" × 6½"
  Fabric 2A: ⅛ yard
  Fabric 3A: ¼ yard
  Fabric 4A: ¼ yard
  Fabric 5A: ¼ yard
  Fabric 6A: ⅜ yard
- 6 gray to black fabrics for block B
  (*fabrics are listed from lightest to darkest*):
  Fabric 1B: 6½" × 6½"
  Fabric 2B: ⅛ yard
  Fabric 3B: ¼ yard
  Fabric 4B: ¼ yard
  Fabric 5B: ¼ yard
  Fabric 6B: ⅜ yard
- Red: 5" × 5" square for apple
- Green: scraps for leaves
- Backing: ¾ yard
- Cotton batting: 27" × 27"
- Binding: ⅓ yard
- Transparent thread
- Various thread colors for appliqué and quilting
- Brown embroidery floss
- Paper-backed fusible adhesive (I use 17"-wide HeatnBond Lite by Therm O Web): 2 yards
- Marking pencils for light and dark fabrics (erasable or water-soluble)
- Masking tape
- White fabric paint

CUTTING

BLOCK A FABRIC	CUT SIZE	NUMBER TO CUT
1A	6½" × 6½"	1
2A	2" × fabric width	1
3A	2" × fabric width	2
4A	2" × fabric width	2
5A	2" × fabric width	2
6A	3" × fabric width	3

BLOCK B FABRIC	CUT SIZE	NUMBER TO CUT
1B	6½" × 6½"	1
2B	2" × fabric width	1
3B	2" × fabric width	2
4B	2" × fabric width	2
5B	2" × fabric width	2
6B	3" × fabric width	3

LOG CABIN BLOCKS

1. Make 1 block A and 1 block B in the courtyard style (page 68). The blocks must be identical so that they can be layered one on top of the other. Use a stitch length of 1.5–2mm.

Block A

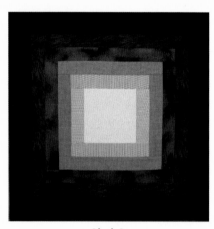

Block B

2. Cut pieces of paper-backed fusible adhesive large enough to completely cover the backs of both blocks. Following the manufacturer's instructions, fuse the adhesive to the wrong sides of both blocks.

Fuse adhesive to blocks.

3. Remove the paper backing from both blocks. (You may want to save it to use as a pressing sheet for another project.)

Weaving the Blocks

1. Place the pre-fused blocks right side up on a cutting mat. With a water-soluble or erasable marking pencil, draw vertical and horizontal center lines on both blocks.

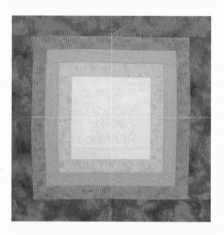

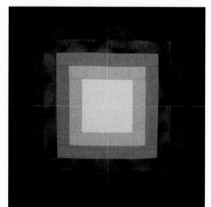

Mark center lines.

2. Attach masking tape on top of Block A, ½" from the top edge (to prevent cutting through this section). Do not cut through the masking tape.

Note

You must cut an odd number of strips. If you cut an even number of strips, you will have opposite colors on the right and left edges of the quilt (in the same row, vertical or horizontal). If your vertical and horizontal center strips straddle the center line of the quilt, you will have an odd number of strips.

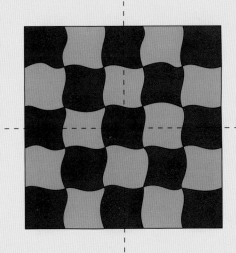

Even and odd numbers of strips in woven quilt

3. Mark straight vertical guide lines on block A with a water-soluble marker. Draw straight lines, as guides for cutting curvy strips. Starting from the central vertical line, draw lines ¾″ to the right and ¾″ to the left; then draw lines 1½″ to the right and 1½″ to the left. Finally, draw lines ¾″ between all vertical

seams on both sides of the center line. Note that the outermost side strips will be ½″ wider than the other strips (on both blocks) so that you can square up the quilt after weaving.

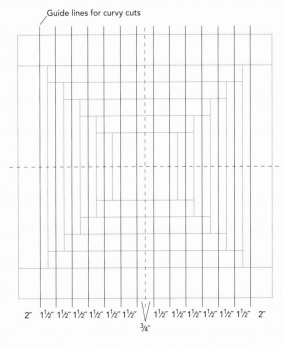

Mark straight vertical guide lines on block A.

4. Following the marked guide lines, use a rotary cutter to freehand cut vertical curvy lines between the seams on each Log Cabin strip and through the Log Cabin center of block A. Cross the drawn straight lines with gentle curves, approximately ½″ to the left and to the right of the lines. Cut from the bottom edge of the fabric toward the masking tape and stop at the tape. (Do not cut through the tape.) You will have a total of 15 strips.

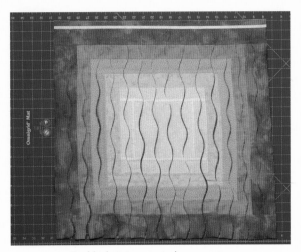

Cut block A into vertical curvy strips.

Note

If you cut through the masking tape by mistake, don't worry. We snip these ends apart later anyway. Just pin them tightly next to each other as if they had never been cut.

5. Mark straight horizontal guide lines on block B using a water-soluble or erasable marking pencil. Use the same distances as for block A (Step 3, page 25). Following the marked guide lines, cut freehand horizontal curvy lines between the seams on each Log Cabin strip and through the Log Cabin center on block B.

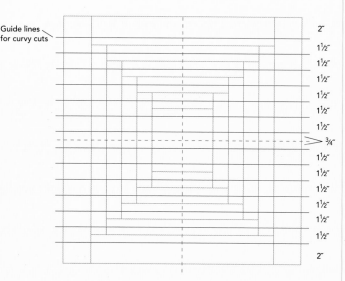

Guide lines for curvy cuts

2″
1½″
1½″
1½″
1½″
1½″
1½″
¾″
1½″
1½″
1½″
1½″
1½″
1½″
2″

Mark straight horizontal guide lines on block B.

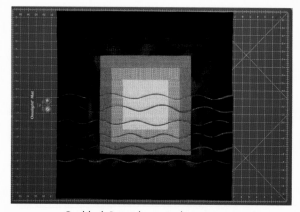

Cut block B into horizontal curvy strips.

6. Place the 27″ × 27″ cotton batting on a weaving pad (page 66). Pin block A (above the masking tape) to the weaving pad, centering the block on top of the batting.

7. Weave the center strip of block B into the horizontal center of block A—over, under, over, under, and so on. Align the center line drawn on the fabric B strip with the horizontal center line drawn across the vertical strips of fabric A. Pin on the sides and anywhere necessary to keep the seams of the Log Cabin blocks aligned.

Note

Align the Log Cabin block seams from strip to strip. Keep the seams aligned by pinning them as you weave.

8. Take the next strip of block B (below the center strip) and weave it into block A below the first strip—under, over, under, over, and so on. Pin at the Log Cabin seamlines to keep them aligned and pin each end of the horizontal strip to the outer vertical strips. Repeat with the third horizontal strip. Continue weaving and pinning the strips. Pin the last horizontal strip on the bottom to the very end of each vertical strip.

Weave from center toward bottom.

9. Rotate the weaving pad 180°. Remove the masking tape and unpin the uncut section at the unwoven end of the vertical strips. Finish cutting the vertical curvy strips by snipping the ends to separate the strips from one another. (See the photo on page 16.)

10. Weave the second half in the same way as you wove the first half.

11. When you are satisfied that all seams are aligned and all the strips fit tightly, follow the adhesive manufacturer's instructions to fuse the woven block to the batting. Keep your iron on a medium setting. Start from the center and press (lift up and down)—do not slide the iron.

12. Remove the pins. Iron again to ensure that the weaving is completely fused.

Fused block

13. Place the quilt top on the cutting mat and trim it to 21½″ × 21½″ square. Finish the raw edges of the woven strips with zigzag stitching (page 67, Option 2) using transparent thread.

APPLIQUÉ

1. Place paper-backed fusible adhesive on top of the apple and leaf patterns on the pullout page (paper side up, adhesive side down) and attach the adhesive with masking tape. The patterns are reversed and ready to trace. Trace them onto the paper side of the adhesive.

2. Cut out the patterns approximately ¼″ outside the drawn lines.

3. Fuse the patterns to the wrong sides of the red and green fabrics.

4. Cut out the appliqué pieces on the drawn lines and remove the paper backing.

5. Position the appliqué pieces on the quilt top. When you are happy with your composition, fuse it to the quilt. Zigzag stitch the edges with matching thread.

6. Hand embroider the stems with 3 strands of brown embroidery floss.

QUILTING AND FINISHING

1. Layer, baste, and quilt. Quilt in-the-ditch of the Log Cabin block seams and around the appliqué using transparent thread. Quilt accent lines on the apple and veins on the leaves using coordinating thread. Finally, use white fabric paint to create a small glimmer of light on the apple. See the photo on page 22.

2. Refer to pages 68–69 for binding instructions.

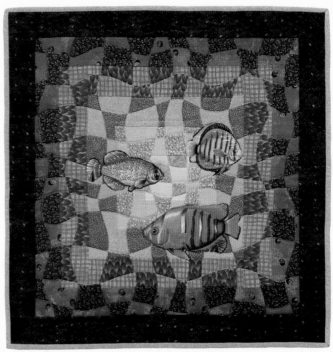

SWIM AWAY by Gert Oest

WHERE DO FAIRIES COME FROM? by Marilyn Korn

Hints

- If you have trouble aligning the seams of the 2 Log Cabin blocks during the weaving, it is because your blocks are uneven. However, don't worry—you can "cheat." Determine which strip needs to move. Cut it in two places—once underneath the overlapping strip to its left and once underneath the overlapping strip to its right. You have now created a short strip that can be aligned without moving the entire long strip, and the cuts will not be visible on the quilt top. Align the seams and pin well.

- If the stitches in a seam start to come apart while you're weaving, place a little white glue on the seam. Let the glue dry and then continue to weave.

- Another option for this quilt is to use pink, lilac, and purple or light blue to navy fabrics in gradated values instead of the black and gray fabrics.

- If you are not confident working with a rotary cutter, practice on scraps of fabric until you are. Remember to always cut away from your body.

Misaligned seam

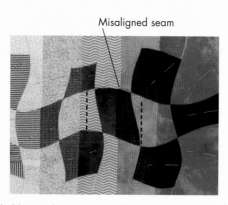

Cut hidden (underneath) part of black strip on dashed lines to create a short strip that can be aligned independently.

Inspiration

LILY POND, 42¼" × 42¾"

Inspiration from a botanical garden

The background of *Lily Pond* is made using the shredded blocks technique beginning on page 22.

I like lilies and have a lot of pictures of them from botanical gardens, so finding the fabric with printed lilies inspired me to make this wallhanging quilt. I made two huge Log Cabin blocks: one with different values of green and the other with white, gray, and black. I cut the blocks into curvy strips, wove them together, and fused on the lilies—they make this quilt look like a pond. I used couching to make the waves in the water.

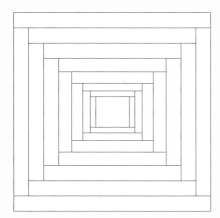
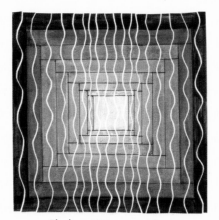
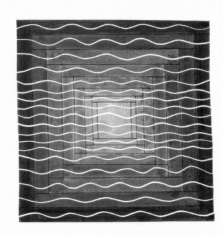

Blocks cut into curvy strips

NIGHT DREAMS, 43″ × 43¾″

Night Dreams represents my own sleepless nights with many thoughts and dreams—like bubbles, they come out slow and pop fast. This quilt is made from two 36″ × 36″ Log Cabin blocks using the shredded blocks technique beginning on page 22. The blocks were constructed with a square in the corner, and the strips were added to the two sides of the square. I also added a wide border. Then, I added the appliqués, embroidery, and couching. I like clowns; they remind me of a cozy childhood and make me calm. I thought that one in pajamas might help me fall asleep.

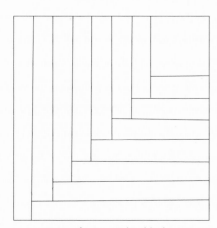

Setting for Log Cabin blocks

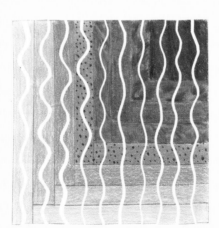

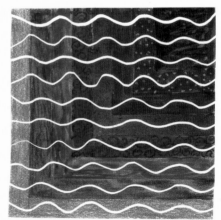

Blocks cut into curvy strips

Blocks cut into curvy strips

ECLIPSE, 32″ × 38″

Solar eclipses happen very rarely, and when they do, people come out to observe and admire the beautiful sight. Parents and neighbors gather with their children to catch the moment, and we can hear little voices asking, "Daddy, why is it getting so dark?" We see little fingers pointing from the shoulders of their fathers as if to make sure that no one misses the darkness turning into light and the magnificent glow from behind the moon.

I made two identical Log Cabin blocks in the courtyard style with a yellow-red and lilac-purple color palette using the technique beginning on page 22. Then I cut two circles—

one orange and one black—and over-painted them for a three-dimensional look. I appliquéd one circle onto each block with zigzag stitching. From the back side of the blocks, I cut away the pieced-block fabric under the appliqué to eliminate the extra layers.

I fused adhesive to the backs of both blocks and cut the blocks in strips, as shown in the picture: one with vertical curvy strips and the other with horizontal curvy strips. (Use the shredded blocks technique beginning on page 22.) When I cut through the circles, I used the parallel and meridian lines of a globe to make the circle look like a sphere. Then, I added the appliqués, borders, and couching.

CHAPTER 3

CIRCLE WEAVING

After I made a few works with the shredded blocks technique, I continued to experiment with fabric strips. I found an interesting way to weave fabric by cutting one fabric into circles, cutting another fabric into wedges, and weaving them together. This weaving technique is similar to basket weaving but is not three-dimensional. The *Color Wheel* project will walk you through the process.

COLOR WHEEL

COLOR WHEEL

Finished quilt size: 21″ × 21″

Color Wheel is an interesting project to make. You will create a small circle-weaving wallhanging. You can add appliqué on top, if you wish.

MATERIALS

Fabric amounts are based on 40″ fabric width.

Prewash all fabrics before use.

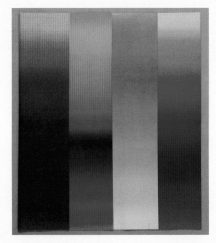

- Colorful fabric(s): 12″ × 22″ pieces of 7 rainbow colors (OR 1¼ yards of a gradated fabric)
- Black: ¾ yard
- Backing: 1 yard
- Cotton batting: 25″ × 25″
- Binding: ⅓ yard
- Transparent thread
- Paper-backed fusible adhesive (I use 17″-wide HeatnBond Lite by Therm O Web): 2 yards
- Colored marking pencils for light and dark fabrics (erasable or water-soluble)
- Masking tape
- Tweezers

CUTTING

Black: Cut a square 22″ × 22″.

Paper-backed fusible adhesive: Cut 3 pieces 22″ × 17″.

WOVEN BACKGROUND

1. Make 2 squares 22″ × 22″ of paper-backed fusible adhesive as follows. Cut 2 strips 22″ × 5¼″ from 1 of the 22″ × 17″ pieces of adhesive. Place the other 22″ × 17″ piece of adhesive, paper side up, on a flat surface. Overlap it by ¼″ with one of the 22″ × 5¼″ strips, paper side up, and secure the 2 pieces with masking tape. Be sure to place the masking tape on the paper side of the adhesive. Repeat with the remaining 22″ × 17″ piece of adhesive and the remaining 22″ × 5¼″ piece.

2. On the paper side of one of the squares of adhesive, draw vertical and horizontal center lines. Trace the circles from the pullout page onto the paper side of the adhesive.

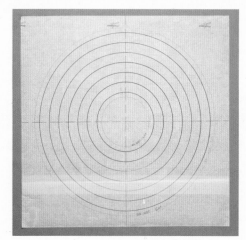

Trace circles onto paper side of adhesive.

3. Fuse the marked adhesive to the back of the black fabric. Leave the paper backing attached.

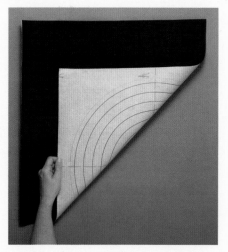

Black fabric with adhesive attached

4. On the paper side of the second square of adhesive, draw vertical and horizontal center lines. Trace the circle that is divided into numbered wedges from the pullout page.

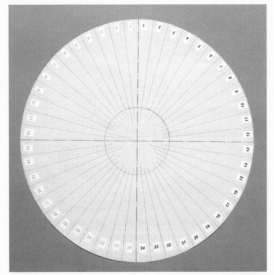

Trace circle divided into wedges onto paper side of adhesive.

The colors are symmetrical on the quilt. The wedge numbers repeat in each half-section of the circle. When you trace the wedges onto the paper side of the fusible adhesive, use one color pencil to mark the wedge numbers for one half-section and another color pencil for the other half. This way you will not inadvertently weave a right-half wedge into the left half or vice versa.

5. Cut the wedges, leaving them attached to the center circle.

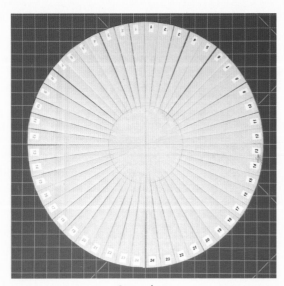

Cut wedges.

6. Match the color of the fabric with the wedge number, as shown in the chart. Cut each paper wedge away from the center circle only when you are ready to fuse it to its appropriate color fabric. This method keeps the wedges in order. Fuse the adhesive wedges to the corresponding fabrics.

COLOR		NUMBER OF WEDGES	WEDGE NUMBERS FOR RIGHT- AND LEFT-HALF SECTIONS OF THE CIRCLE
	Blue	4	Right: 1, 2 Left: 1, 2
	Green	10	Right: 3, 4, 5, 6, 7 Left: 3, 4, 5, 6, 7
	Yellow	8	Right: 8, 9, 10, 11 Left: 8, 9, 10, 11
	Orange	8	Right: 12, 13, 14, 15 Left: 12, 13, 14, 15
	Red	8	Right: 16, 17, 18, 19 Left: 16, 17, 18, 19
	Violet	4	Right: 20, 21 Left: 20, 21
	Purple	6	Right: 22, 23, 24 Left: 22, 23, 24

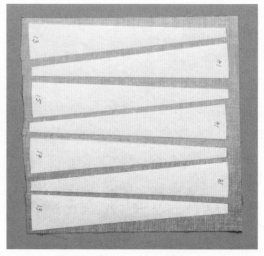

Fuse wedges to colored fabrics, matching wedge numbers with colors.

As you cut the fabric into wedges, keep the fused wedge you are cutting under the ruler. Do not move the ruler around the outside edges of the wedge. Instead move the wedge around underneath the ruler to align the edges. This technique will help you to cut your wedges more accurately.

7. Cut out the fabric wedges. Leave the paper backing attached.

8. Pin the fused black fabric onto a weaving pad (page 66), paper side up. Slide a cutting mat between the weaving pad and the first half-section of the black fabric and cut on the 7 black circle lines. Start and end your cuts 1″ beyond the center line. Do not cut on the red lines; they are guide lines. Gently remove the paper backing from 6 half-circles one-by-one (from only half of the weaving area), cutting the paper backing, *not the fabric*, at the red center guide lines. Remove the cutting mat.

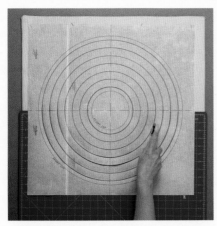

Cut 7 circle lines 1″ beyond center line.

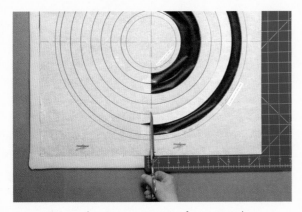

Snip and remove paper strips from cut circles.

9. With the adhesive sides of both fabrics up, weave the wedges into the background fabric. Remove the paper backing from each wedge right before you weave it into the circles. Start weaving at the red vertical center line. Weave both sets of wedges numbered 1 to 12 into the circles. Start with wedge number 1 on the left, then weave wedge number 1 on the right, number 2 on the left, number 2 on the right, and so on. Weave from the outer circle toward the center: over, under, over, under, and so on.

10. All of the wedge inner ends should be on top of the red center circle. The wedge outer ends should be on top of the red outer circle line. Pin each end. Keep the woven wedges tight in the intersections. Remember to weave in the numbered order shown on the wedges.

Begin weaving.

11. When you finish weaving half of the quilt, rotate your work 180°. Slide the cutting mat between the weaving pad and the unfinished part of the circle. Cut the rest of the circle lines and remove the paper backing (Step 8).

12. Weave the wedges from 13 to 24, one on the left side then one on the right side, continuously, in numbered order, until all the wedges have been woven.

Note

Use tweezers to help you weave the last few wedges.

Use tweezers to weave last few wedges.

If you have space between the wedges, pull them gently toward the center, a little bit over the red center circle, while gently pushing the black circles away from the center.

Note

If you don't have enough space left to put in the last wedge, pull all of the wedges approximately ⅛" away from the center red circle, toward the outer edge past the outer red circle, while holding the black circles in place.

The wedges are wider on one end, so by pulling them toward the center, you make them fit more tightly, and by pulling them away from the center, you make them fit more loosely.

The last big woven circle should be close to the outer red circle; adjust it with your fingers and pin it in place.

13. When you are satisfied, remove the pins from the small center circle. Cover the whole weaving with leftover paper backing from adhesive, shiny side

down (or use a Teflon pressing sheet), and iron the woven circle to fuse the weaving together so it can be moved. Remove the rest of the pins during the ironing process.

Note

If your leftover paper backing or pressing sheet is not large enough to cover the entire weaving, iron part of the weaving, let the backing or pressing sheet cool, and then carefully reposition it so that it is always between your iron and the adhesive.

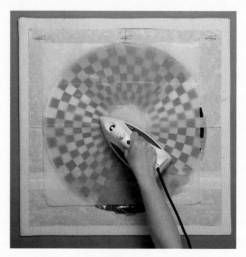

Ironing

14. Let the paper backing or pressing sheet cool and then remove it.

Note

If you don't have the leftover paper backing or a pressing sheet, you can center the cotton batting over the woven circle and iron it with high heat until the woven circle is securely attached to the batting.

15. Turn the woven circle right side up and center it on top of the 25″ × 25″ cotton batting. Remove the paper backing from the remaining unwoven black outer circle and unwoven small center circle. Position them as shown.

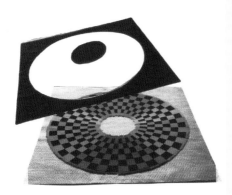

Assemble quilt top.

16. Pin them in place and fuse them to the batting on top of the woven circle. Remember to press by lifting up and down; *do not slide the iron.*

17. Square up your quilt to 21½″ × 21½″. Finish the raw edges of the woven strips with zigzag stitching (page 67, Option 2) using transparent thread.

QUILTING AND FINISHING

1. Layer, baste, and quilt. Quilt in-the-ditch of the woven strips using transparent thread.

2. Refer to pages 68–69 for binding instructions.

I LOVE QUILTING by Charlene R. Van Gurp

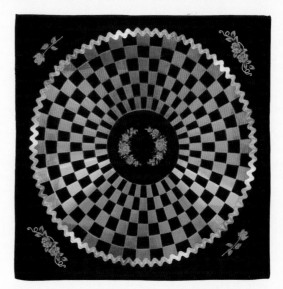

THE ROSES AROUND by Harriet Hollema

BOOP BOOP DE DOOP by Patti Rabe

MY ROOSTER CALLED ISY, 47" × 46½"

In 2005, we celebrated my husband Isy's sixtieth birthday. I made a quilt for him, which I titled *My Rooster Called Isy*. In the Eastern calendar, twelve animals represent a cycle of twelve years, one for every year. My husband was born in the year of the rooster, and I tried to design a special rooster with the characteristics of my husband: pride, caring, and honesty, with true colors.

I used a black fabric for the background circles and a colorful piece of fabric with a gradation of colors from turquoise to blue, green, and yellow using the circle weaving technique beginning on page 32.

This quilt is very dear to me because right after my husband's birthday it won a prize at the New Jersey Quilt Convention, and I was awarded a Bernina sewing machine.

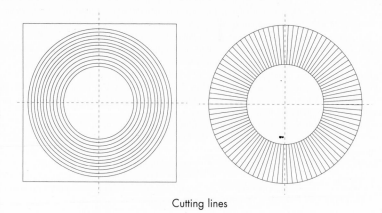

Cutting lines

Wedges fused to gradated fabric

MORE
POSSIBILITIES

Be sure to read the first three chapters of this book, which give you much of the information you will need to understand and experiment with the following weaving techniques. Have fun with the endless possibilities for weaving quilts. I hope you are a curious quilter with artsy cells in your blood and that you find that my quilts have no secrets and are an open creative road for you.

Note

Iron paper-backed fusible adhesive to the back of each piece before you cut it into strips or circles for weaving. Always remove the paper backing before weaving. Work with the fabrics right side up for weaving, unless instructed otherwise. Fuse the woven quilt top to batting and finish the edges with zigzag stitching. Add appliqué and then quilt and bind.

CHAPTER 4

SEMI-CIRCLE WEAVING
(BANANA SHAPED)

Inspiration

PROUD FEATHERS, 45" × 45³⁄₄"

We were in Brazil one February—the month of Carnival. While there, I was inspired by the thousands of feathers, mostly peacock feathers, that decorated the beautiful costumes. Another year, when we were in Portugal, I was intrigued by the live peacocks in a large courtyard in a port wine factory we visited. It was exciting to see the peacocks showing their brightly colored tails opened as a fan. They looked as proud as peacocks.

For *Proud Feathers*, I used two quilt-size circles of fabric. One was made by sewing together a purple print and lighter purple print. The other was in tie-dyed yellow and orange.

I fused adhesive to the backs of both circles. On the paper-backed side of the yellow-orange fabric, I drew a 40"-diameter circle with a 20"-diameter circle and an 18"-diameter circle in the center. I divided the circle into 38 wedges. Then I created a banana-shaped template and used it, right side up, to draw banana-shaped lines 38 times around the circle. (To make it easier for you here, I have divided the circle into quarters and each quarter into 9 wedges, for a total of 36 wedges and 36 banana shapes.) I cut out and removed the 18" circle to reduce the bulk in the center.

On the purple fabric, I drew a 40"-diameter circle with a 5½"-diameter circle in the center. I divided the circle into the same number of sections as the yellow-orange circle and drew banana-shaped lines with the template *wrong* side up. The result was that I had banana-shaped designs on both fabrics, but the designs were going in opposite directions, one curving clockwise and the other counterclockwise.

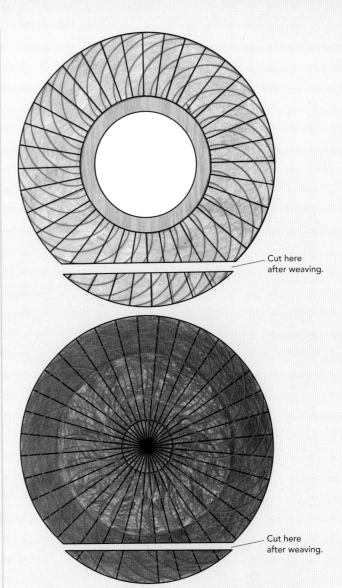

Cut here after weaving.

Cut here after weaving.

Cutting lines drawn on two parts curve in opposite directions.

I cut on the curved drawn lines (shown in red) and removed the paper backing. Then I placed both fabrics right side up on top of batting on a weaving pad (page 66), with the purple circle on top of the yellow-orange circle, and I wove the two fabrics together.

When I was satisfied with the result, I fused the woven piece to the batting and cut a section off the bottom. Then I cut and fused other fabrics in complementary colors on the background around the bird tail. I fused and machine appliquéd the bird and the details in the tail.

I finished the raw edges by zigzag stitching with clear transparent thread and couched decorative yarn (page 67). I machine embroidered the bird and the details in the tail. I embellished the feathers with beads, rhinestones, and couching. I quilted in the weaving lines on the tail, and I stipple quilted on and around the bird with free-motion machine quilting. I used fabric markers to add details to the bird feathers.

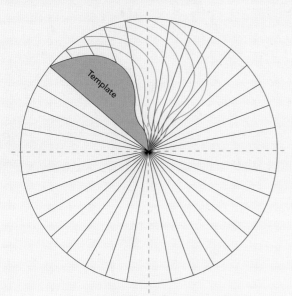

Draw banana-shaped lines with template.

CHAPTER 5

CIRCLE CURVY WEAVING

Inspiration

CHEER UP CLOWN, 42″ × 43¾″

Isn't it always exciting to have a good laugh, see some miracles, and be cheered up when you are upset or moody? Even memories of good times can change your mood from dark to bright in the blink of an eye. The circus is a subject that always works for me. I like the beautiful costumes, the rhythm of the performance, and the continuous movements, projecting lights, bright colors, glitter, sparkles, crying and laughing clowns, magic, and miracle music—all in this make-believe world.

I designed *Cheer Up Clown* in a circle. I wanted to show the movement of colors and the rhythm of music.

I made this quilt with the circle curvy weaving technique (similar to the circle weaving technique beginning on page 32) because curvy lines are more playful than straight lines.

I fused adhesive to the back of a wallhanging-size piece of black fabric and drew a circle in the center of the fabric for the appliqué. Then I divided the circle into 48 wedges, extending the wedge lines to the fabric edges. Starting from the center circle, I cut the 48 freehand curvy lines with a rotary cutter.

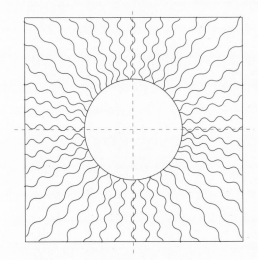

Cut curvy wedges on paper-backed side of black background.

Next, I created a large panel of paper-backed fusible adhesive, the same size as the black background fabric, by taping pieces of adhesive together on the paper sides. I drew center vertical and horizontal lines. I labeled the top (T) and bottom (B) and the left (L) and right (R) sides of the panel and then drew 10 concentric circles and labeled them T, B, L, and R also. I drew freehand curvy lines over the circle lines.

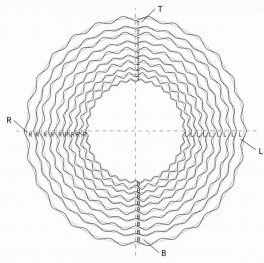

Draw and label curvy lines.

I cut curvy circles from the adhesive panel and fused them to 9 different fabrics—one circle for each fabric.

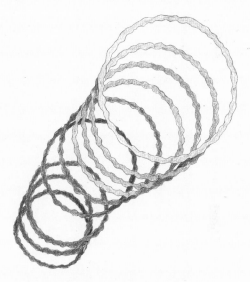

Fuse, then cut curvy circles from different fabrics.

I removed the paper backing and wove the curvy circles one-by-one into the black fabric, starting with the smallest circle, matching the vertical and horizontal center marks, and pinning the circles securely.

After I finished weaving, I fused everything to the batting, including the floppy ends of the curvy black strips in the corners. To finish the raw edges, I used zigzag stitching and couching (page 67). I created the appliqué on leftover paper backing from the adhesive and then fused and machine appliquéd the appliqué to the center of the quilt. I free-motion machine quilted the piece.

I drew the face with colored pencils.

CHAPTER 6

DIAGONAL WEAVING

Inspiration

In *Come With Me*, the people walking together in the park on a rainy fall day seem to be inviting others to join them— someone in the group says, "Come with me."

All the figures in this quilt, except two, are made from a special fabric that looks either black or silver-blue depending on how you look at the quilt. When you look at it straight on, the figures under the umbrellas look like black silhouettes; but when you look from the side, all the figures disappear, except for one sweet couple walking in the rain.

COME WITH ME, 31" × 41¾"

To create this quilt, I made one big (wallhanging-size) Log Cabin-style block. I cut this block into horizontal strips, except for a square in the upper right corner, which I left whole.

Cutting lines for diagonal strips

Quilt panel made as Log Cabin-style block

I fused the woven quilt top to batting and then added the appliqués. I finished all of the raw edges with zigzag stitching using clear transparent thread (page 67), except for the raw edges of the leaves in the tree. I left the raw edges of the leaves unfinished and stipple quilted them. I added the borders and finished the quilt with free-motion quilting and binding.

Panel cut into horizontal strips, except for square in upper right corner

Silhouettes of people disappear.

CHAPTER 7

COMBINATION WEAVING

Inspiration

I really love cats! They have lived in my heart all my life. I treat them as human beings. They are smart, beautiful, and funny, and, believe me, they know what they are doing. Every one has a special character and body shape, gorgeous honest eyes, fur in natural colors, and a tail to express itself. Most of them have a hot temper, but they know how to behave, if they have to. If they are hungry, cats will give you the most tender, loving look in the world. Some day they will start talking to me—I'm still waiting.

I really enjoyed the process of creating this quilt, especially drawing and painting the cat image. This quilt combines straight and diagonal weaving with straight and curvy strips, using the simple curvy weaving technique beginning on page 12. I cut one panel from a piece of eggshell-colored fabric, cut partially into strips (one section at a time). For the second panel, I used four fabrics, which were cut into strips and woven into the first layer.

I DIDN'T DO IT, 42½″ × 49″

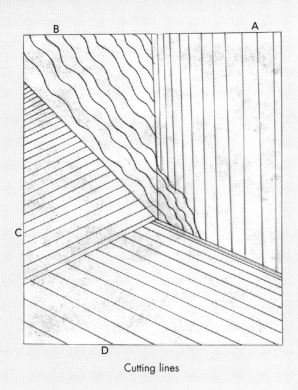

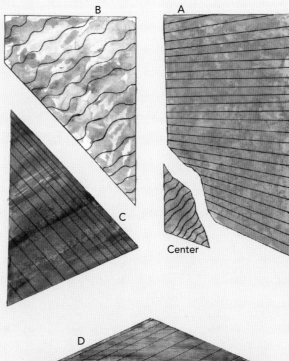

Cutting lines

Center

D

Cat for appliqué

I fused the woven quilt top to the batting and finished the raw edges with zigzag stitching (page 67).

Referring to a photograph of my cat, I drew the cat on a piece of beige and brown cotton fabric using pastel chalks and fabric paints.

I painted, cut out, and fused all of the remaining appliqué details onto the quilt and then did the quilting.

Inspiration

WAITING FOR GRANDPA, 34¼″ × 45″

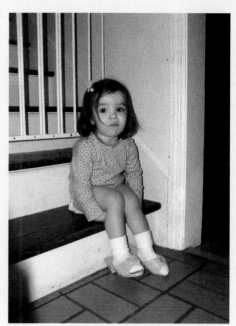

Courtney

My husband handed me this picture and said, "Make a quilt." The eyes and facial expressions revealed, with no doubt, that Courtney was upset about something serious. Perhaps she was worried that her older sister would find out she had taken her Cinderella shoes.

As the work progressed, my husband couldn't take his eyes off her face. "Look at her! You could just hug and kiss her!" Somehow you simply wished that you could change that sad face into a smiling one. Finally the quilt was completed, and the task of giving it a title began. "What shall we call it?" "Oh, I don't know!" "You made it, you name it." "No, you asked me to make it, you name it."

How about *Waiting for Grandpa*? Yes! That's it. Certainly Grandpa will put a smile on her face.

First, I painted the entire quilt on one piece of fabric. I used Setacolor textile paints from Pro Chemical & Dye. These fabric paints are very friendly on fiber and easy to use. It was a pleasure for me to draw and paint such a cute face. Then I cut three foreground and background sections—around Courtney, the steps, and the flowers—into strips of various shapes.

I cut a blue, pink, and green stripy fabric into vertical strips and wove the strips into the background of the quilt above the flowers, using the simple curvy weaving technique beginning on page 12. (Although some of the strips were cut straight, the technique is the same.) Then I cut and wove the floor and the background on the right side of the flowers.

A

B

C

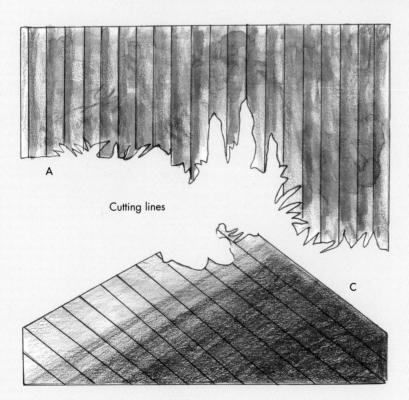

A

Cutting lines

B

C

CHAPTER 8

COMBINATION OF SHREDDED BLOCKS AND CIRCLE CURVY WEAVING

Inspiration

SPRING IS IN THE AIR, 34³/₄" × 56"

Cutting lines for black fabric

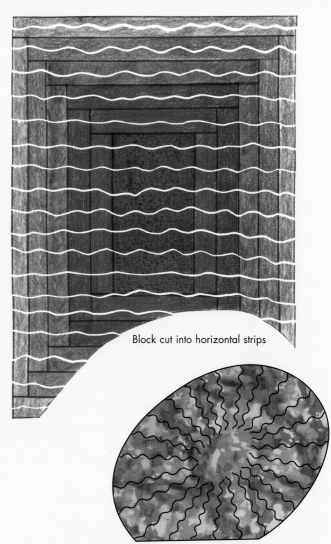

Block cut into horizontal strips

Cutting lines for colorful fabric

When I look at this quilt, images and thoughts of spring abound. I see children coming out of school, laughing and jumping, picking the first flowers to bring home for their moms. I see youngsters taking their bicycles for rides, and lovers in the park kissing and expressing their feelings at the first sign of the warm sun. I see seniors walking and holding hands. The clown celebrates all that's going on. I can see spring in his eyes, too. He rides, he laughs, and he yells to everyone: "Spring is in the air!"

To make this quilt, I cut a quilt-size piece of black fabric for the background, and I cut an oval from a colorful fabric. Using purple fabrics of various values, I made a Log Cabin block, starting with a dark rectangle in the center and adding lighter fabrics as I moved toward the sides.

I fused adhesive to the backs of all three pieces and cut them into curvy strips and curvy circles.

I did the weaving using the simple curvy weaving and shredded blocks techniques beginning on pages 12 and 22. I fused the woven quilt top to batting. Then I appliquéd the clown on the unicycle, the balloons, and the flowers.

I made the clown on leftover paper backing from fusible adhesive. First, I fused adhesive to all the pieces of the appliqué. Second, I removed the paper backing from the pieces, arranged the detailed image on the shiny side of leftover paper backing, and fused the composition together. I gently peeled the clown from the paper backing, fused it to the quilt, and stitched it on.

I finished the edges on the woven parts using zigzag stitching, and I couched around the appliqué with various yarns (page 67). I also couched the clown pants, to make the colors stand out. I free-motion stipple quilted in and around the multicolored oval. I quilted in the weaving lines in the Log Cabin block.

CHAPTER 9

PARTLY CURVY WEAVING

Inspiration

NIGHT WATCH, 40¼" × 45¼"

Cutting lines

One day after our Empire Quilters guild meeting, I came home with my friend Sandra Samaniego, and we spoke about our love of wolves. We both agree with those who believe that other living things are our equals, with a right to existence. Sandra said that we should not destroy nature, that we can live in harmony, and that all creatures are necessary for this planet to survive.

After that talk, I decided to make a wolf quilt. I wanted to show wisdom in his eyes, passing from one generation to another. I wanted to show the wolf as a symbol of freedom. This wolf, in his wild, frozen woods, makes me count my blessings.

To begin, I chose two pieces of fabric: a decorative sateen fabric with a light gray print (also used for the binding) and a plain white cotton. I fused paper-backed adhesive on the back of both fabrics. I painted both of the fabrics with the same image of the woods but in a different palette of colors. After letting the paintings dry and heat setting them, I cut the background piece into vertical curvy strips, using the simple curvy weaving technique beginning on page 12. I left the middle part uncut for the image of the wolf. I cut the second piece into vertical curvy strips and wove them into the background piece.

I fused the woven quilt to the batting and then painted the wolf in the middle of the quilt. I used acrylic paint, oil pastels, and colored pencils. To make the trees and bushes look three dimensional, I couched them with yarn using zigzag stitching and clear transparent thread (page 67). I used transparent yellow fabric for the moon appliqué, and zigzag stitched around it. It was the smallest appliqué I've ever done. I finished my quilt with free-motion machine quilting.

CHAPTER 10

CIRCLE AND SPIRAL WEAVING WITH TWO HAND-PAINTED FABRICS

Inspiration

DISCO, 40¾" × 49½"

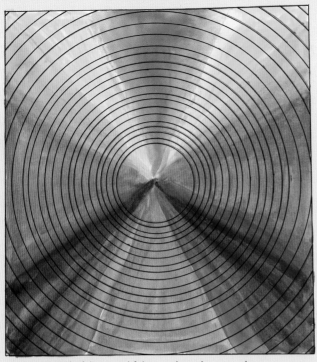

Colorful painted fabric with circle cutting lines

Monochromatic painted circles with wedge cutting lines

I love to use rainbow colors, but sometimes I have trouble finding the right fabrics, so last year I started painting fabrics for my quilts.

Disco was inspired by the Kylie Minogue song "Can't Get You Out of My Head." I like the song, but one day I couldn't get it out of my head. As the melody and words played in my head over and over, I said to myself, "I have to make a quilt—maybe it will distract me."

I painted one fabric in many different sections of colors, symmetrically around the vertical center line. I drew four large circles on a second piece of fabric and painted them in different values from white to gray and black (dark next to light and light next to dark). I couldn't imagine how the painted panels would look when I wove them into one quilt. I applied fusible adhesive to both painted panels, and I marked cutting lines: circles on the colorful background, and 64 wedges on the monochromatically painted fabric.

I wove this quilt using the circle weaving technique beginning on page 32. I was really surprised by the results. As you can see, the combination of light and dark monochromatic colors with a colorful background makes a strong visual impact. The circles look as if they are floating above the quilt. I added a painted border at the bottom, couched lines in the center and along the wedge lines, and machine quilted.

ON TOP OF THE QUILTED WORLD, 42″ × 45″

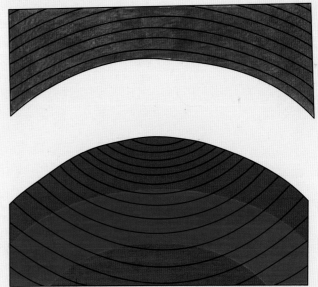

Painted panels with cutting lines

Everybody knows how important it is to be inspired before you start to make a quilt. The Pegasus is a symbol of inspiration for art creativity. When I am inspired by something, I don't count the hours and days. I like to just follow the idea or project and forget about all problems, troublesome situations, and complications. And I can tell you one secret—this Pegasus likes to visit me quite often.

The first version of this quilt depicted a Pegasus in my backyard, but I thought that he shouldn't be just for me; he had to be for everybody around the earth and in the sky, and especially for quilters. So I made another Pegasus quilt and named it *On Top of the Quilted World*.

I used two quilt-size panels of sateen fabric. On one, I painted different colors in repeated arcs across the fabric. The other, I cut into two shapes, one for the sky and another for the earth, and I painted the sky in purple and the earth in purple, red, and navy.

I fused paper-backed adhesive to the fabrics, then cut wedges on the background panel. Then I cut semi-circles one-by-one from the sky and earth fabrics and wove the semi-circles into the background, using the circle weaving technique beginning on page 32.

I fused the appliqué, covered the entire quilt top with tulle, and then couched the Pegasus image with gold yarn and clear transparent thread (page 67). Finally, I free-motion machine quilted the entire surface.

DON'T BUG ME, 45″ × 48½″

Background fabric with circle cutting lines

Second fabric with wedge cutting lines

Usually, I start thinking about spring at the end of January, when the days become noticeably longer and the sun starts looking brighter. In February, the red colors of Valentine's Day are visible, soon to be complemented by the greens of nature. When birds begin to celebrate spring and the first flowers show their beautiful buds, I want to be a part of it. I decided to make a quilt that combines, in one big flower, the colors of all of the spring flowers and a lot of ladybugs. These little creatures in red with polka dots look really great on green grass. I like to put them on the palm of my hand, make a wish, and gently blow on them to make them fly away.

On two 44″ × 44″ squares of white fabric I drew identical images of one big flower. I painted one flower in red, purple, pink, and emerald green, and the other in yellow, orange, hot red, green, and blue. When the paint was dry, I heat set it for permanence. I fused adhesive to the backs of both fabrics.

I chose the panel with yellow and blue for the background and drew circles on the paper-backed side of the panel.

I marked the center of the other panel. I drew one circle and divided the rest of the fabric into 64 wedges, extending the dividing lines to the edges of the panel.

Then I wove the pieces together using the circle weaving technique beginning on page 32. I fused the completed woven quilt top to the center of a piece of cotton batting that was large enough to add borders.

I completed the flower by fusing on appliqué details. The blue inner border and the green outer border are fused to the batting. The whole quilt is covered with a navy-colored tulle (page 67) and free-motion machine quilted on the weaving lines. To finish the quilt, I fused 23 hand-painted ladybugs on top of the tulle cover and stitched around their raw edges. I then couched black yarn around the flower petals with zigzag stitching and clear transparent thread (page 67). The free-motion quilting on the ladybugs was done last.

MY SECRET PLANET, 46″ × 56″

When you look at the sky on a starry night, you don't see any color—you see only deep darkness, sparkling stars, some slow-moving satellites, and the moon. For people on earth, space is ageless. We know the past and the future are there, but it is difficult to imagine eternity. Spectacular pictures taken through a space telescope with a special lens show beautiful, fantastic colors: stars, planets, and space itself. When we look at these objects from earth, we just have to believe they are colorful.

Some pictures of space and the stars in *Sky & Telescope* magazine were the inspiration for *My Secret Planet*. I wanted to combine the familiar

terrestrial image of a snail's shell with the strange eternity of space. I imagined a secret planet—my place to escape for a while from the everyday routine. There I can dream, relax, be inspired, enjoy the polychromatic colors of my little planet, and contemplate a view of earth and space.

I made this quilt using a spiral weaving technique similar to the circle weaving technique beginning on page 32. I used two pieces of white cotton fabric and cut them into identical shell shapes with 2″ of extra fabric around the edges. I painted one shell with wedges of luminescent colors, and the other with a spiral in black, gray, and white.

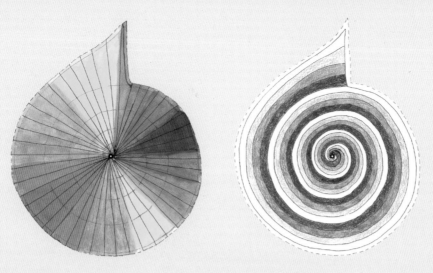

Cutting lines

After the paint was dry, I fused adhesive to the backs of both shell panels. On the paper-backed side of the colorful panel, I drew 46 wedges from the center to the sides (I eyeballed it). I divided the monochromatic panel with four spiral lines.

I cut the monochromatic shell panel on the spiral lines, pinned it, paper-backed side up, to a weaving pad (page 66), and removed the paper. I cut the colorful shell panel on the wedge lines and wove the wedges one-by-one wrong side up into the monochromatic spiral, starting from the entrance to the shell (at the top).

When the weaving was done, I fused the woven image to the shiny side of leftover paper backing from fusible adhesive, removed the paper, and fused the shell right side up to a large piece of batting. I covered the shell image with thin tulle (page 67). I over-painted two fabrics slightly: a black fabric with printed planets and a black fabric with printed stars. I cut two pieces from each print for a total of four pieces (each piece approximately ¼ of the quilt size). I pieced them together in a huge four-patch and then cut the shell image from the center, 2″ smaller all around than the woven spiral shell. I also pieced a small border strip for the bottom. I used basting spray on the batting around the shell image and placed the top of the quilt on top of the batting and the spiral. I reverse appliquéd the top to the woven image using zigzag stitching and couching with yarn and clear transparent thread (page 67). I also fused some details on top of the quilt and the border. I quilted with free-motion machine quilting.

Pieced background with appliqué and border

Reverse appliqué

CHAPTER 11

FUZZY WEAVING

Inspiration

ENIGMA, 47" × 47"

Background panel with cutting lines for fuzzy echo strips

Second panel divided into wedges

Ecological problems become current and closer to us every day. The first and most important problem for all the world's people is obtaining clean resources like air and water. For my quilt *Enigma*, I created an image of a drop of water, which possesses life energy, represented by the randomly drawn red rays.

The red and green colors are symbols of heat and life. The black layers are like approaching threats encircling the space. This quilt is an expression of the fight between good and evil, between dark and bright powers, between healthy living bacteria and the heavy chemical junction around my, so far still barely clear, drop of water.

I painted two panels of fabric using complementary colors: for the background panel, I used yellow, orange, red, and purple; and for the other panel, yellow-green, emerald, and blue.

After the paint dried, I fused adhesive to the entire back of the background panel and to the painted parts of the second panel. With the paper-backed side up, I cut half of each curve in the smallest painted curvy image on the background panel, removed the paper from the cut sections, and pinned the panel to the weaving pad (page 66) wrong side up.

I divided the second panel into wedges drawn on the paper-backed side, using the middle of the water drop as the center point. I cut the wedges from the background, one-by-one, the smallest wedge first, removed the paper backing, and wove them into the cut half of the smallest curvy image around the water drop. (I used the circle weaving technique described beginning on page 32.)

Next, I slid a cutting mat under the other half of the curves of the smallest curvy image on the background panel and cut them. I removed the cutting mat and the rest of the paper backing and then finished weaving the wedges into this first curvy image. I repeated all the steps with the rest of the surrounding layers and in the corners. When the weaving was done, I covered it with batting and fused it all together.

I turned the quilt top right side up, covered it with tulle (page 67), and added the black-and-white printed fabric appliqué. I then couched some of the curvy lines with yarn (page 67), and I free-motion machine quilted on the weaving lines with stippling between the woven parts.

STRESS, 29¼" × 29¼"

Cutting lines

Cutting lines for fuzzy echo strips around face

The quilt *Stress* was made in memory of the terrible disaster on 9/11, when we all learned what stress means. We all knew the world would never be peaceful again. Women are extremely sensitive to any danger; it affects our physical and mental health and our behavior.

I designed my image of stress, which shows a woman analyzing, remaking, and reconsidering negative information and thoughts inside an overloaded stressed brain. I designed these thoughts as straight, sharp, and pointy—long, curvy, and annoying.

You can see this whole process in the woman's eyes. This small wallhanging has a lot of details but only one image, the face.

I used two 21″ × 21″ squares of fabric and painted two identical portraits in different colors: one monochromatic black, gray, and white, and the other polychromatic turquoise, blue, navy, purple, magenta, and red.

After the paint dried, I fused adhesive to the backs of both portraits. I removed the paper backing and pinned the colored portrait right side up to batting on a weaving pad (page 66). I slid a cutting mat under the fabric and freehand cut the fuzzy echo strips around the face.

From the monochromatic portrait, I cut long, curvy strips around the face one-by-one and wove them in a clockwise direction into the pinned colored portrait. Then I cut the colored face into fuzzy horizontal strips and the other face into fuzzy vertical strips and wove the two sets of strips together. I fused the woven portrait to the batting, then added all the appliqué details and the painted borders. Then I covered the whole quilt with tulle (page 67).

I couched some appliqué pieces with gold yarn and clear transparent thread (page 67) and then free-motion machine quilted.

BASIC INSTRUCTIONS

Hints

- I prewash all of my fabrics before using them.
- I use Wonder Invisible Thread for my transparent thread. It is 100% nylon and doesn't melt when ironed.
- Practice cutting strips with a rotary cutter on scrap fabric until you are comfortable and confident. Always cut away from your body.
- Use all-metal pins that can be ironed over. Always iron your woven piece again after all the pins have been taken out, to ensure that every bit of the weaving is fused and to remove any pin marks.
- Remove all marking pencil lines before ironing. The heat can set them and make them difficult to erase.
- Let your creativity and artistic freedom have free rein. Change my instructions, square up a quilt to any size you like, use colored thread instead of transparent…Experiment and have fun!

During the weaving process, the warp and weft cross each other in an over under, over under progression.

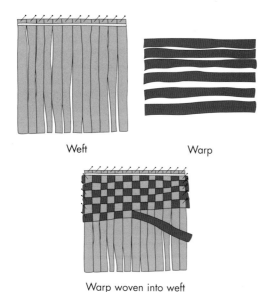

Weft   Warp

Warp woven into weft

WEAVING PAD

I use a homemade weaving pad for my weaving. It's extremely easy to use; you can pin your work to it, iron on it, and move it to another place. Attaching batting to the pad under the weaving makes the weaving more stable, so the weaving process is easier and more accurate. You can also use the pad for ironing; I recommend putting it on top of the ironing board before you iron.

To make a weaving pad:

1. Cover one side of a 24″ × 24″ × 2mm piece of Masonite with a thin layer of white glue.
2. Center a 24″ × 24″ piece of felt or fleece over the glued Masonite, smoothing out any wrinkles with your hands. Let the glue dry.
3. Center a 28″ × 28″ piece of cotton or linen fabric on top of the pad.
4. Turn the pad over and fold and glue the 2″ of extra fabric to the back of the pad on all 4 sides, mitering the corners.
5. Glue a 23″ × 23″ square of fabric to the back of the pad to cover the raw edges. Let the glue dry.

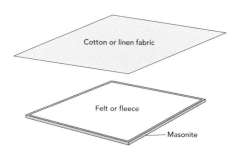

Cotton or linen fabric

Felt or fleece

Masonite

Place glue, felt or fleece, and fabric on Masonite.

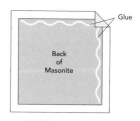

Glue

Back of Masonite

Fold fabric to back.

Back fabric cover

Miter corners.   Cover back with fabric.

FINISHING EDGES OF WOVEN STRIPS

There are three ways to finish the raw edges of the woven strips.

Option 1

Fuse all appliqué to the quilt top. Cover the front of the quilt top with fine navy or black tulle and pin the layers together. Add thread embellishment to the appliqué over the tulle, including any satin stitching or couching.

Spray baste the backing to the layered quilt top and batting. Using clear transparent thread or decorative quilting thread, machine quilt on the weaving lines of the background and elsewhere as desired.

Place tulle over weaving, and quilt on weaving lines.

Option 2

Using transparent or matching thread, finish all the raw edges in the background with tiny zigzag stitching on the weaving lines through the quilt top and the batting. Fuse all appliqué to the quilt top and add thread embellishment to the appliqué, including any satin stitching or couching.

Pin or spray baste the backing fabric to the quilt top and batting. Machine quilt as desired, using clear transparent thread or decorative quilting thread.

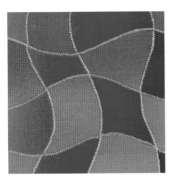

Finish raw edges of woven strips with zigzag stitching.

Note

If you don't mind seeing zigzag stitching on the back of your quilt (and if you don't intend to enter your quilt in a judged show), you can add the appliqué before you layer the quilt top and batting with the backing; then finish the raw edges of the weaving lines with zigzag stitching when you are machine quilting.

Option 3

Fuse all appliqué to the quilt top and add thread embellishment to the appliqué, including any satin stitching or couching. Use zigzag stitching and transparent thread to couch decorative yarn to finish all the raw edges of the woven strips on the background. Since the lines on which you are couching are not continuous, you will have tails of couched yarn to hide. Thread the tails on a needle and pull them to the back of the quilt top. They will then be sandwiched inside the quilt when you add the backing.

Pin or spray baste the backing fabric to the quilt top and batting. Machine quilt as desired, using clear transparent thread or decorative quilting thread.

Finish raw edges by couching with yarn.

LOG CABIN BLOCK, COURTYARD STYLE

Use ¼″ seam allowances.

Note

See page 23 for cutting instructions.

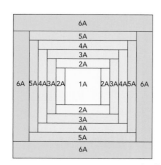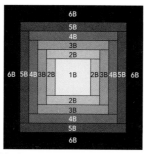

Finished blocks

1. For block A, sew two 2A strips onto opposite sides of the 1A square. Trim the strips even with the square. Press the seam allowances away from the square. (Pressing arrows are included in the diagrams.) Repeat for block B with the 1B square and two 2B strips.

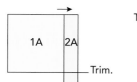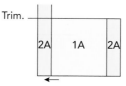

Stitch, trim, and press.

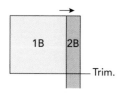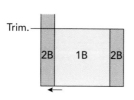

Stitch, trim, and press.

2. Sew two 2A strips to the top and bottom of the block. Trim the strips even with the edges of the block. Press. Repeat for block B with two 2B strips.

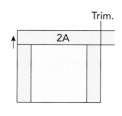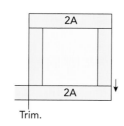

Stitch, trim, and press.

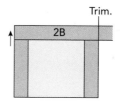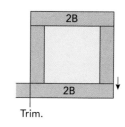

Stitch, trim, and press.

3. Repeat Steps 1 and 2 with fabrics 3–6, sewing 2 strips to the sides of blocks A and B and then 2 strips to the tops and bottoms of the blocks, until you have 5 strips on each side of the center square of both blocks.

DOUBLE-FOLD STRAIGHT-GRAIN BINDING (FRENCH FOLD)

1. Trim excess batting and backing from the quilt. If you want a ¼″ finished binding, cut the binding strips 2¼″ wide and piece them together with diagonal seams to make a continuous binding strip. Trim the seam allowances and press the seams open.

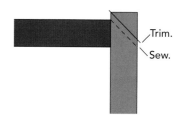

Stitch diagonal seams and trim.

Press open.

2. Press the entire strip in half lengthwise with wrong sides together and raw edges even.

3. Align the raw edges of the binding with the raw edges of the quilt top. Pin the binding to the edge of the quilt, starting a few inches away from a corner. Leave the first several inches of the binding unattached. Start sewing, using a ¼″ seam allowance.

4. Stop ¼″ away from the first corner and backstitch one stitch.

Stitch to ¼″ from corner.

5. Lift the presser foot and needle. Rotate the quilt one-quarter turn. Fold the binding at a 45° angle, so that it extends straight above the quilt.

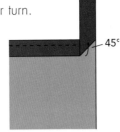

First fold for miter

6. Fold the binding strip down, even with the top and side edges of the quilt. Begin sewing at the folded edge.

Second fold alignment

7. Repeat in the same manner at all the remaining corners.

Finishing the Binding

Choose between these two methods for finishing the binding.

Method 1

1. Open the end of the binding strip and fold it under ¼". Press.

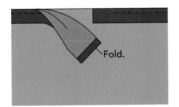

Fold binding end under ¼".

2. Refold the strip on its original lengthwise fold to get a finished edge on this end of the binding strip.
3. Place the beginning binding strip on top of the ending strip that has the folded edge.
4. Trim the excess from the beginning binding strip about ½" beyond the folded edge of the ending strip.

5. Continue stitching the overlapped binding strips to the quilt.

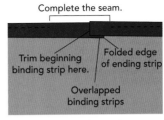

Overlap strips and complete seam.

6. Fold the binding over the raw edges to the quilt back and hand stitch the binding to the back, mitering the corners.

Method 2

1. Fold the ending tail of the binding back on itself where it meets the beginning binding tail.
2. From the fold, measure and mark the cut width of the binding strip. Cut the ending binding tail to this measurement. For example, if your binding is cut 2¼" wide, measure 2¼" from the fold on the ending binding tail and cut the binding tail to this length.

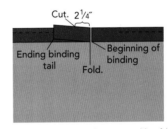

Fold and then cut binding tail to cut-width of binding.

3. Open both tails. Place one tail on top of the other tail at right angles, right sides together. Mark a diagonal line and stitch on the line. Trim the seam allowance to ¼". Press the seam open.

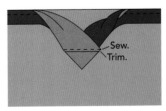

Stitch ends of binding diagonally.

4. Refold the binding on its original lengthwise fold and finish sewing the binding to the quilt.
5. Fold the binding over the raw edges to the quilt back and hand stitch the binding to the back, mitering the corners.

About the Author

Anna was born in Saint Petersburg, one of the most beautiful cities in Russia. This gorgeous city sits on five islands. There are 500 bridges over canals and rivers, beautiful cathedrals, churches, parks, and gardens. The "white" summer nights are very special—the sun does not go down, and the sunset turns into sunrise.

Anna found her talent at a very young age. When she was only eight years old, she started to paint water-color copies of classic reproductions. Her paintings were naive, but colorful. She liked to paint swans in the lake and make furniture for her dolls from paper and scraps of fabric, gluing them together. After high school, she wanted to be either an art teacher or a doctor, but the urge to create remained strong.

Upon graduating from college, she taught art to first through eighth grade students, acted as a stage and costumes decorator at the Kirov Theater of Opera and Ballet, and as a freelancer, knitting and designing sweaters.

Anna loves to work with textiles, threads, and other fiber media. She has a passion for creating art quilts. She has developed a few new techniques; some of them are presented in this book, and she is saving others for future books.

In 1995, she traveled to the United States to visit her sister and was lucky enough to obtain a green card and the absolute freedom and subsequent inspiration that come with it.

For more information, ask for a free catalog:
C&T Publishing
P.O. Box 1456
Lafayette, CA 94549
(800) 284-1114
email: ctinfo@ctpub.com
website: www.ctpub.com

For quilting supplies:
Cotton Patch Mail Order
Cotton Patch
1025 Brown Ave.
Lafayette, CA 94549
(800) 835-4418 or
(925) 283-7883
email: CottonPa@aol.com
website: www.quiltusa.com

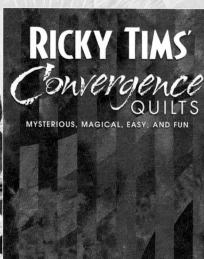